STARS OF
WORLD
SOCCER

Abbeville Press Publishers

New York · London

A portion of the book's proceeds are donated to the **Hugo Bustamante AYSO Playership Fund**, a national scholarship program to help ensure that no child misses the chance to play AYSO Soccer. Donations to the fund cover the cost of registration and a uniform for a child in need.

Text by Illugi Jökulsson

For the original edition
Design: Ólafur Gunnar Guðlaugsson
Layout: Ólafur Gunnar Guðlaugsson and Árni Torfason

For the English-language edition
Editor: Nicole Lanctot
Production manager: Louise Kurtz
Layout: Ada Rodriguez
Copy editor: Mike O'Connor

PHOTOGRAPHY CREDITS

Getty Images: p. 6 (Buda Mendes), 17 (Shaun Botterill), 33 (Christof Koepsel)

Shutterstock: p. 8 (Marcos Mesa Sam Wordley), 9 (Kriengsak Talek), 10 (Marcos Mesa Sam Wordley), 11 (Maxisport), 13 (Celso Pupo), 15 (AGIF), 18 (AGIF), 20 (AGIF), 21 (360b), 22 (mooinblack), 27 (Maxisport), 28 (mgilert), 29 (Celso Pupo), 31 (Maxisport), 32 (AGIF), 35 (AGIF), 37 (katatonia82), 38 (Jefferson Bernardes) 39 (Marcos Mesa Sam Wordley), 40 (AGIF), 42 (YiAN Kourt), 44 (fstockfoto), 46 (Natursport), 48 (AGIF), 50 (AGIF), 51 (American Spirit), 52 (AGIF), 55 (Matt Trommer), 56 (AGIF), 58 (Natursport), 60 (AGIF), 61 (Maxisport)

Wikimedia Commons: p. 14 ("C-bob" by Source. Licensed under fair use via Wikipedia)

Árni Torfason: p. 25

First published in the United States of America in 2015 by Abbeville Press, 116 West 23rd Street, New York, NY 10011

First edition
10 9 8 7 6 5 4 3 2 1

Library of Congress Cataloging-in-Publication Data

Illugi Jvkulsson.
 Stars of world soccer / by Illugi Jvkulsson. -- First edition.
 pages cm
 Audience: Age: 7.
 ISBN 978-0-7892-1239-9
 1. Soccer players--Biography--Juvenile literature. I. Title.
 GV942.7.A1I455 2015
 796.334092'2--dc23
 [B]
 2015013376

For bulk and premium sales and for text adoption procedures, write to Customer Service Manager, Abbeville Press, 116 West 23rd Street, New York, NY 10011, or call 1-800-ARTBOOK.

Visit Abbeville Press online at www.abbeville.com.

CONTENTS

Agüero was for a time married to Giannina Maradona, the youngest daughter of Diego Maradona, one of the world's greatest soccer players. They have one son.

Back home in Argentina, Agüero is called "Kun" due to his childhood resemblance to a cartoon character named Kun.

AGÜERO

Explosive Energy, Boldness

Every soccer player dreams of scoring a goal at the pivotal moment in a final, but that dream comes true only once in a blue moon. Sergio "Kun" Agüero will probably never forget when he scored such a goal for Manchester City in the final game of the 2011–2012 season of the English Premier League.

Heading into the final games of the season, both Manchester teams, City and United, had an equal number of points, and soccer fans around the world gathered to watch the tantalizing culmination.

United were leading against Sunderland at halftime and Queens Park Rangers were ahead against City at the end of normal playing time. As a result, it seemed like United would defend their title and become English champions for the 13th time in 20 seasons. However, Agüero prevented this from happening. During injury time, Edin Džeko scored an equalizer and then Agüero scored the winning goal a few moments later, just seconds before the referee blew the whistle. City became champions for the first time in 44 years. Agüero was the hero.

Agüero played his first game with Independiente in Argentina when he had just turned 15 years old, becoming the youngest-ever player in the Argentinean league.

After playing a few years in his home country, Agüero was purchased by Atlético Madrid in Spain, and when an Arabian billionaire bought Manchester City and decided to turn it into a superpower, Agüero was one of the players they wanted.

Agüero has flourished with Manchester City and now counts among the world's fiercest goal scorers. Whatever team he plays for, Agüero gravitates toward the goal.

He is a part of a fantastic generation of Argentinean geniuses who helped the national team snatch the Olympic gold medal in Beijing in 2008. Lionel Messi has reached furthest of these talented Argentineans, and in addition to Agüero, it is also worth mentioning Angel Di María. They were runners-up at the 2014 World Cup in Brazil and may have taken home gold if Agüero hadn't suffered an injury at a critical moment.

SERGIO "KUN" AGÜERO
STRIKER
ARGENTINA

BORN JUNE 2, 1988
IN BUENOS AIRES, ARGENTINA
HEIGHT 5'8"
PLAYED FOR INDEPENDIENTE
(ARG), ATLÉTICO MADRID
(ESP), AND MANCHESTER CITY
(ENG)
INTERNATIONAL GAMES 59
GOALS 22

GARETH BALE
WINGER/FORWARD
WALES

BORN JULY 26, 1989
IN CARDIFF, WALES
HEIGHT 6'
PLAYED FOR SOUTHAMPTON
(ENG), TOTTENHAM (ENG), AND
REAL MADRID (ESP)
INTERNATIONAL GAMES 49
GOALS 16

When Bale was a schoolboy, he was so good at soccer that his physical education teacher had to set special rules that applied only to him. He was restricted to playing one-touch soccer and not allowed to use his favored left foot.

BALE

The Welsh Powerhouse

The world of soccer is sometimes strange. On September 1, 2013, the 24-year-old Welshman Gareth Bale became one of the most expensive soccer players in history when Real Madrid purchased him from Tottenham Hotspur in England for $112 million. At the time, Bale had neither won a title with his club nor competed in a significant tournament with the Welsh national team. However, it is a clear mark of Bale's talent that when he was bought by Real Madrid, no one was surprised about Real's interest in acquiring him, even if some people might have frowned at the price.

The fact that Bale played for long at left back sets him apart from other forwards. From early childhood, Bale exhibited vast talent, and it was clear that he would become a great athlete. At the tender age of 16, Bale played his first game with the English Premier League team Southampton. Bale began scoring goals right away, though mainly from free kicks.

A year later, Tottenham bought the young Bale and placed him on defense. However, he soon progressed up the field, where his speed and attacking spirit could be put on display. Bale has tremendous shooting abilities, he is acutely skilled in getting past defenders, and his speed is almost beyond belief.

During his final season with Tottenham, Bale scored 26 goals in 44 games. Nowadays, Bale mostly plays out on the right, where his incredible crossing ability can shine, but sometimes he simply plays as a lightning-quick forward.

With Real Madrid, Bale must fight for the limelight with the genius Cristiano Ronaldo. However, Bale has proven his worth and is an important asset to the fantastic Real team.

Bale is famous for his "heart" goal celebration. He has registered it as a trademark.

KARIM BENZEMA
STRIKER
FRANCE

BORN DECEMBER 19, 1987
IN LYON, FRANCE
HEIGHT 6'2"
PLAYED FOR LYON (FRA) AND
REAL MADRID (ESP)
INTERNATIONAL GAMES 76
GOALS 25

BENZEMA

The Ultimate Goal

The big European soccer clubs are constantly searching for young and talented players. The younger, the better. Karim Benzema was only nine years old when Lyon announced their interest in having him join their ranks. At that time, he played with his hometown club Bron Terraillon. Initially, Bron resisted and refused to let him go, but eventually Benzema was allowed to undergo a trial period with Lyon. Benzema ultimately switched clubs.

Benzema was born and raised in the suburbs of Lyon, France, but he traces his roots to Algiers. Benzema was a diligent young boy; he exerted himself at practices, did well in school, and served as a ball boy during the Lyon club's home games. From early on, Benzema was a talented goal scorer, and he racked up goals in the youth league. He played his first game with the senior team in 2004. Lyon was a superior club in France around that time and was in the midst of a string of seven straight championship years. Slowly but surely Benzema gained prominence on this fiercely strong team.

He has a relentless knack for entering the penalty area at the right time and knows exactly the right place to drive the ball into the net.

During the 2007–2008 season, Benzema became champion with Lyon for the fourth time, was the top goal scorer in the French league, and was chosen as the league's best player.

The following year, Benzema was transferred to the Spanish giants Real Madrid. His inaugural year proved a struggle, but Benzema applied himself and quickly became a more versatile striker. He has by now claimed all the important accolades with Real and he is still in his prime.

Early in his career, Benzema was accused of lacking focus. The famous coach José Mourinho made it clear to Benzema that mere talent would not be enough for him to succeed with Real Madrid; he would need to develop his skills through hard work and practice.

COSTA
Unyielding Fighting Spirit

We are all familiar with stories of soccer players who exhibited great promise at a very young age and were then signed with big teams before even finishing high school. The story of Diego Costa is different. He was 15 when he attended his first soccer practice. Costa, who is named after the Argentinean genius Diego Maradona, played soccer with his friends on the streets of his home city of Lagarto, Brazil. There was no local soccer club in Costa's old neighborhood; there wasn't even a soccer field to play on. In order to succeed on the streets, agility was not enough, toughness was just as important.

Costa began attending soccer practices after his family moved to São Paulo, Brazil, and only two years later he was a full-fledged professional player in Portugal. From 2006, Costa played with a few clubs in Portugal and Spain. In 2010, he joined the ranks of Atlético Madrid, where he served as backup for the dangerous forwards Sergio Agüero and Diego Forlán.

In the 2012–2013 season, Costa was at the front rank of the Atlético squad, alongside Radamel Falcao, and the team became Spanish champions for the first time in 18 years. Costa was the top scorer for Atlético that year, and the club went on to fight for the title in the UEFA Champions League final.

Following his stint with Atlético, Costa signed a contract with Chelsea, and he began the 2014–2015 season in full force. Costa scored seven goals in his first four league games and by the end of February, he had scored 19 goals in 26 games. During the same period, Costa was given nine yellow penalty cards as well as a three-match ban for a stamp missed by the match officials.

Diego Costa is hard as nails and he feels no need to apologize for it.

Every Brazilian boy's biggest dream in life is to wear the yellow shirt of the national team. This dream came true for Diego Costa when he played two friendly games for Brazil in 2013. And even in this field, Costa traveled his own path. From there on he decided to play for the Spanish national team and he seemed unscathed by the animosity this created in Brazil.

DIEGO COSTA
STRIKER
SPAIN

BORN OCTOBER 7, 1988
IN LAGARTO, BRAZIL
HEIGHT 6'2"
PLAYED FOR ATLÉTICO MADRID
(ESP) AND CHELSEA (ENG)
INTERNATIONAL GAMES 7
GOALS 1

LUIZ
Passionate Defender

In the summer of 2014, David Luiz became the most expensive defender in history, as the English Premier League club Chelsea sold him to the French club Paris Saint-Germain (PSG) for $77 million—a price usually reserved for the most sought-after goal scorers. Some contended that the deal was a brilliant move for the colorful Chelsea coach José Mourinho, since the burden of a controversial and inconsistent defender was relieved, for a record amount of money. And people shook their heads at the new owners of PSG from Qatar, who were thought to have been duped.

Even though David Luiz is sometimes unpredictable, there can be no doubt that when in his top form, he is a driven, passionate, and clever defender. He also has the ability to score elegant goals from free kicks or from a distance.

Luiz has played for the Brazilian national team since 2010. Unfortunately, his most memorable game may be the seven-goal defeat at the hands of the German national team during the 2014 World Cup. Luiz was team captain and failed in his efforts, like the rest of the Brazilian team. After the game, Luiz famously fell into tears in an interview with reporters. However, despite this disappointing loss, Luiz has retained his position as captain, and he is passionate about rebuilding the Brazilian team.

David Luiz is often called Sideshow Bob due to his resemblance to the frizzy-haired character from *The Simpsons*.

**DAVID LUIZ
DEFENDER
BRAZIL**

**BORN APRIL 22, 1987
IN DIADEMA, SÃO PAULO,
BRAZIL
HEIGHT 6'2"
PLAYED FOR BENFICA (POR),
CHELSEA (ENG), AND PARIS
SAINT-GERMAIN (FRA)
INTERNATIONAL GAMES 47
GOALS 3**

DE GEA

Inner Strength

It goes without saying that no amateur could be expected to replace the famous goalkeeper Edwin van der Sar of Manchester United or the equally celebrated Iker Casillas of the Spanish national team. Many were named, but David De Gea was the one chosen.

De Gea trained with his local team in Madrid and then joined Atlético's youth academy when he was 13. In fact, some subterfuge was involved in the process: De Gea's former coach lied to Atlético club officials, telling them that another team was about to sign the young goalkeeper. Regardless, Atlético concluded that De Gea was a promising talent and there was too much at stake. They decided to sign him as a result and there was no regret.

De Gea played with the youth squads of the Madrid team and all younger divisions of the Spanish national team. After a stint defending the goal for the Atlético reserve team during the 2008–2009 season in the Spanish third division, De Gea was approached by a number of clubs interested in acquiring him on loan. Atlético officials encouraged De Gea to transfer, but he refused and was consequently barred from training as punishment. De Gea trained by himself for a while and eventually attracted the attention of the Atlético manager, who offered him the chance to train with the first team and become the third-string goalkeeper. Before long, De Gea was the starting goalkeeper for the team and contributed to their 2009–2010 UEFA Europa League championship.

In 2011, De Gea signed a contract with the reigning English champions, Manchester United. It took some time for De Gea to find his feet with the new club. Some claimed that Alex Ferguson, the manager of United, had made a mistake by signing such a young and inexperienced goalkeeper. Nonetheless, De Gea showed them what he was made of and Ferguson's decision was proven solid.

Now it's simply a matter of time before De Gea will take over from Casillas as the starting goalkeeper for the Spanish national team.

Fans of De Gea's goalkeeping count his inner calm and strength as his major virtues. If De Gea makes a mistake, he makes sure it will not be repeated. He learned from his thorny beginnings with United, and he won game after game for his team during the 2014–2015 season.

DAVID DE GEA
GOALKEEPER
SPAIN

BORN NOVEMBER 7, 1990
IN MADRID, SPAIN
HEIGHT 6'4"
PLAYED FOR ATLÉTICO MADRID
(ESP) AND MANCHESTER
UNITED (ENG)
INTERNATIONAL GAMES 3

ANGEL DI MARÍA
ATTACKING MIDFIELDER/
WINGER
ARGENTINA

BORN FEBRUARY 14, 1988
IN ROSARIO, ARGENTINA
HEIGHT 5'10"
PLAYED FOR BENFICA (POR),
REAL MADRID (ESP), ROSARIO
(POR), AND MANCHESTER
UNITED (ENG)
INTERNATIONAL GAMES 57
GOALS 11

DI MARÍA
The King of Assists

It is not often that children are prescribed soccer by a doctor, but such was the case with Ángel Di María. He was an energetic child with a great need to be active, and as a result, his parents were advised to send him to practice soccer so he would get the outlet he required. It's reasonable to assume that Di María's parents never suspected that 20 years later he would become one of the world's greatest soccer players.

Di María is extremely skillful both on the wing and behind the strikers, and his precision passes are eye-catching.

Di María played with Rosario Central in the city of his birth. The club is one of the major teams in Argentinean soccer, surpassed only by the big teams in the capital, Buenos Aires. Di María played two seasons with the club before he was bought by Benfica in Portugal, where he would win three titles.

In 2010, Di María transferred to Real Madrid, a team that would become league champion, Spanish champion, and winner of the UEFA Champions League during Di María's tenure. Manchester United bought Di María in 2014 for the highest amount that any English club has paid for a player, making Di María the sixth most expensive player in soccer history.

Di María was on the under-20 Argentinean national team that became world champions in 2007 and on the under-23 team that took home the Olympic gold in 2008.

Di María scored his first goal for the senior national team in the 2010 World Cup. He was one of the team's key players, and his excellent performance gave the team confidence that he would succeed at the 2014 World Cup. Unfortunately, Di María suffered a serious thigh injury during a game in the 2014 World Cup quarterfinal and was therefore absent in the semifinal game against the Netherlands and in the final, in which Argentina was defeated by Germany. Many believe that his presence would have led to Lionel Messi, captain of the Argentinean team, raising the trophy instead of German captain Philipp Lahm.

> Only two months after the 2014 World Cup final, the Argentineans exhibited what could have happened had Di María been in full health. The Argentinean team played a friendly match with the newly crowned world champions from Germany and won a secure 4–2 victory. Di María assisted on three of Argentina's goals and scored the fourth himself.

MARIO GÖTZE
ATTACKING MIDFIELDER
GERMANY

BORN JUNE 3, 1992
IN MEMMINGEN, GERMANY
HEIGHT 5'9"
PLAYED FOR DORTMUND (GER)
AND BAYERN MUNICH (GER)
INTERNATIONAL GAMES 41
GOALS 13

GÖTZE
Promise of More To Come

Mario Götze is still quite young, but he has already won almost all possible accolades, both with clubs and with the national team. Götze began his career with the German team Dortmund at a young age, and the team won two Bundesliga titles and one DFB Cup with Götze, all before his 20th birthday. Götze was transferred to Bayern Munich before the 2013–2014 season, much to the dismay of Dortmund fans, and he has helped his new team win two Bundesliga titles and one DFB Cup. He has now bagged even more accolades with Bayern. With both Dortmund and Bayern, Götze manifested his growing genius as a dangerous and agile attacking midfielder and playmaker.

Götze has also starred in international play. He was a member of the 2014 World Cup champion team in Brazil and scored the only goal in the final against Argentina, breaking the stalemate in extended time with a beautiful winner in the 113th minute. Few young players have experienced such a wondrous career.

Despite his successes, some people believe that Götze is yet to fully express his true talents. The modest but occasionally flashy German has so much to offer, and so far the world has only seen half of it. Good things can therefore be expected from Götze, because in his short career he has already achieved miracles. He has it all: speed, technique, dribbling skills, and playmaking capabilities. And he can also play as a "false 9," or second striker.

When German coach Joachim Löw sent Götze to the field as a substitute during the 2014 World Cup final, he told him to "show the world that he is better than Messi." And in that one game, at least, he did.

German legend Franz Beckenbauer has described Götze as the "German Messi" for his speed and style of play.

EDEN HAZARD
WINGER/ATTACKING
MIDFIELDER
BELGIUM

BORN JANUARY 7, 1991
IN LA LOUVIERE, BELGIUM
HEIGHT 5'8"
PLAYED FOR LILLE (FRA) AND
CHELSEA (ENG)
INTERNATIONAL GAMES 53
GOALS 6

HAZARD

Flair and Power

It was evident from early on that Eden Hazard's path would lead toward soccer. His parents were fairly successful soccer players: his mother was a striker for the Belgian women's first division and his father played as a defensive midfielder in the Belgian men's second division. Hazard's three younger brothers undertook the same journey.

Hazard was born in La Louvière, a city in the French-speaking part of Belgium. At the age of four, Hazard attended his first practice with his hometown club, where he remained for the next eight years, until he transferred to a more powerful team. When he was 14, Hazard signed with Lille in France, and there he played in the club's youth academy for two years.

At 16, he ascended to Lille's senior team, and as he grew as a soccer player, so did his role in the team. Hazard was twice named Young Player of the Year, and he was named Player of the Year for the 2010–2011 season, following Lille's league and cup victories, and then again for the 2011–2012 season. In 2012, Hazard was purchased by Chelsea, which, earlier in the same season, had won their first UEFA Champions League.

Hazard is one of many fantastic Belgian soccer players who have taken the stage in recent years. The Belgian national team was considered likely to perform well at the 2014 World Cup. However, the team was knocked out in the quarterfinal round with a loss to Argentina.

Hazard nevertheless continues to attract attention for his attacking spirit and agility. When Hazard is at his best, he is capable of magic, and he can deliver passes equaling the ones of Lionel Messi. Hazard's goals and assists both contribute to the winning ways of Chelsea under the auspices of José Mourinho.

Both of Hazard's parents were soccer players. His mother, a gifted striker, only stopped playing when she was three months' pregnant with him. He has three younger brothers, and as of 2015 two of them had already become professional soccer players.

ZLATAN

King in Many Nations

Zlatan Ibrahimović is a true master. He has played with six different clubs in four countries aside from his home country, and he has won championships with all of them. Zlatan—known by his first name—is truly like no other. He is unique, regardless of whether he is on the field or off it.

Zlatan was born in the Swedish city of Malmö, where his parents met. His parents were both Yugoslavian immigrants, his father from the country now known as Bosnia and Herzegovina and his mother from Croatia. When push came to shove, Zlatan could choose to play with three different national teams, but he chose Sweden.

As a youngster, Zlatan played with a few clubs in his hometown. By the age of 15, Zlatan had become unsure about his future in soccer, and he was close to quitting the sport to pursue work at the Malmö docks. So the story goes, anyway. Nevertheless,

Zlatan continued playing soccer and began playing with the senior team Malmö FF when he was 17. The news of his tremendous skill as a goal scorer quickly spread around Europe, and before long, Zlatan was acquired by the Dutch club Ajax in 2001. Ever since, Zlatan has traveled from one big club to the next, racking up goals and collecting titles and fame along the way.

Zlatan was a mischievous adolescent and he has always behaved in a manner unlike other adults. He has argued and sometimes fought with referees and companions and has blurted out various seemingly arrogant comments. Regardless of how you look at it, Zlatan is never dull. And his genius on the field is unarguable, as the countless titles and accolades prove.

> Despite Zlatan's height and bulky build, he is extremely agile, and he has scored numerous goals in a style that would put men with a more elegant physique to shame. See for example his spectacular bicycle kick for Sweden against England in 2013, which won the FIFA Puskás Award for goal of the year.

ZLATAN IBRAHIMOVIĆ
FORWARD
SWEDEN

BORN OCTOBER 3, 1981
IN MALMÖ, SWEDEN
HEIGHT 6'5"
PLAYED FOR MALMÖ (SWE),
AJAX (HOL), JUVENTUS (ITA),
INTER MILAN (ITA), BARCELONA
(ESP), AC MILAN (ITA), AND
PARIS SAINT-GERMAIN (FRA)
INTERNATIONAL GAMES 101
GOALS 51

INIESTA

The Maestro of the Passing Game

For years, Andrés Iniesta has been admired and revered by fans of Barcelona. However, on July 11, 2010, he scored the winning goal against the Netherlands in the World Cup final in South Africa, and he was worshipped across all of Spain as a god.

As a key player on the powerful Barcelona team since 2004 and, since 2006, on Spain's national team, Iniesta is one of the most triumphant players of all time. His track record is impressive: six Spanish league championships, two cup championships, three victories in the UEFA Champions League, two UEFA Super Cup titles, two wins at the FIFA Club World Cup, twice European champion with Spain, and once world champion! His individual accolades and titles are vast.

Iniesta was 12 when he was invited to play in the youth academy of Barcelona, the famous La Masia, and he has remained with the club ever since. Iniesta is exceptionally gifted, his ball control is superior to most players, he directs pinpoint-accurate passes, and he maintains incredible oversight and control of the game. When Iniesta and his companion Xavi were in their top form, both with Barcelona and with the Spanish national team they developed an immaculate reciprocal understanding that made them the greatest midfield pair the world has seen. With Barcelona, Lionel Messi saw to the goal scoring while Xavi and Iniesta maintained their legendary passing game. Over the years, Iniesta's coaches, his companions, his opponents, and experts alike have agreed that he is one of a kind, and many are at a loss when it comes to appropriate superlatives. "Magnificent" and "perfect" are the words that are most often expressed, and they seem applicable.

Iniesta is a composed and calm player, and sometimes his presence on the field is quiet, but his opponents all take a deep breath when he receives the ball, because Iniesta is entirely unpredictable. Nevertheless, they do know that it is near impossible to wrench the ball from him.

> Iniesta learned the lessons in Barcelona's youth academy by heart, where everything revolves around the mantra, as Iniesta himself claims: "Receive, pass, offer, receive, pass, offer."

ANDRÉS INIESTA
ATTACKING MIDFIELDER
SPAIN

BORN MAY 11, 1984
IN FUENTEALBILLA, SPAIN
HEIGHT 5'7"
PLAYED ONLY FOR BARCELONA
(ESP)
INTERNATIONAL GAMES 102
GOALS 12

TONI KROOS
MIDFIELDER
GERMANY

BORN JANUARY 4, 1990
IN GREIFSWALD,
EAST GERMANY
HEIGHT 6'
PLAYED FOR BAYERN MUNICH
(GER) AND REAL MADRID (ESP)
INTERNATIONAL GAMES 57
GOALS 9

The Castrol Performance Index, the official statistical analyzer of the World Cup, rated Kroos as the best player at the 2014 World Cup, with a rating of 9.79 out of 10.

KROOS
The "Waiter" Delivers

"A near perfect player," was the grade given by Dutch soccer legend Johan Cruyff to Toni Kroos following the 2014 World Cup in Brazil. Reviews don't get much better than that, in light of the fact that nobody is perfect. And especially when the compliment comes from someone like Cruyff, who was as close to being a perfect player as anyone in the past four decades.

Toni Kroos's performance at the World Cup was superb throughout but peaked during the historic match between Germany and Brazil, when the world-champions-to-be crushed the hosts 7–1. Kroos scored two goals in the game and had one assist. With Germany's World Cup victory, Kroos was the first ever player from the former East Germany to become world champion.

Kroos played with Hansa Rostock before scouts from the German giant Bayern Munich set their sights on him and offered him an opportunity to join the club. Kroos played his first game in the Bundesliga on September 26, 2007, becoming the youngest player to play with Bayern's senior team, which went on to claim the league championship that season. Kroos was in and out of the lineup for a while, and he joined Leverkusen in 2009 on a loan contract in order to train with their first team. He returned to Bayern for the 2010–2011 season and was twice more league and cup champion as well as being part of the winning team in the 2013 UEFA Champions League.

In 2010, Kroos played in his first international game. After a superb performance at the 2014 World Cup in Brazil, he was transferred to Real Madrid, where he has maintained his stride and played close to flawless soccer.

Kroos's passing accuracy and attacking spirit, as well as his oversight and composure on the field, make him a dangerous weapon for any team. Kroos can be expected to lead Germany's midfield and offensive play for years to come.

At the 2014 World Cup, Kroos was nicknamed Garçom ("waiter" in Portuguese) by the Brazilians for the precision passes he delivered to the German strikers.

MASCHERANO
Fighting Spirit and Cunning

The distinction of any given player's presence on the field obviously varies. To some extent it depends on the player's position, but style of play and the composition of the team also play a considerable role. One could claim that Javier Mascherano is the greatest unnoticeable player in the world.

Surrounded by the stars on Barcelona, he plays the significant role of breaking the opponent's offense and hastily delivering the ball to his teammates, who will often immediately initiate the offensive strategy. And Mascherano plays this part with deliberation, cunning, and unwavering fighting spirit.

The Argentinean's career is quite interesting. He was chosen to be part of the Argentinean national team before he went professional; he became an Argentinean champion with River Plate in 2004 but then made the surprising move of transferring to Brazil. That was an uncommon path for an Argentinean to travel around that time. Mascherano was Brazilian champion with Corinthians in 2005. It was common knowledge that the larger European teams were interested in Mascherano, and in 2006 he joined West Ham in England. West Ham had struggled in the Premier League up to that point, and before long it came to light that West Ham might not own the rights to Mascherano at all. As a consequence, he signed a contract with Liverpool. From there, his journey took him to Barca, where Mascherano was intended to play a modest role. He was mainly set to strengthen a large group of players, but soon he was one of the key players on the team and he has played his part in the club's triumphant march in recent years.

Mascherano has made significant contributions to the Argentinean national team and is one of the most tenured players in the team's history. With the national team, he won the Olympic gold medal in 2004 and 2008 and played in the World Cup in 2004, 2010, and 2014. Argentina came in second during the 2014 World Cup, losing the final to Germany. After the tournament, geniuses such as Lionel Messi, Ángel Di María, and Sergio Agüero covered the headlines, but many insisted that Mascherano had been the prime motor of the team.

Mascherano won two consecutive gold medals at the Olympic Games—in Athens in 2004 and in Beijing in 2008. It is a rare event that a soccer player acquires two Olympic medals.

JAVIER MASCHERANO
DEFENSIVE MIDFIELDER/
DEFENDER
ARGENTINA

BORN JUNE 8, 1984
IN SAN LORENZO, SANTA FE,
ARGENTINA
HEIGHT 5'7½"
PLAYED FOR RIVER PLATE
(ARG), CORINTHIANS (BRS),
WEST HAM (ENG), LIVERPOOL,
(ENG) AND BARCELONA (ESP)
INTERNATIONAL GAMES 110
GOALS 3

LIONEL MESSI
FORWARD
ARGENTINA

BORN JUNE 24, 1987
IN ROSARIO, ARGENTINA
HEIGHT 5'7"
PLAYED ONLY FOR BARCELONA
INTERNATIONAL GAMES 96
GOALS 45

Messi scores goals in all manner of ways. For example, he is a perfect shot with both legs. The classic "Messi goal" takes place following a dribble through a maze of defenders.

MESSI
The Supreme Genius

Only a handful of players in the entire span of soccer history can fall under the heading of "greatest players of all time." Lionel Messi is one of them and probably the name that is most commonly mentioned in discussions about the best of the best. His talents border on the supernatural.

Messi's story is amazing. At the age of five, he began playing soccer under the guidance of his father, who coached the boys in the neighborhood. At age eight, Messi moved to a larger team, Newell's Old Boys, which had better facilities and more structured practices. When Messi was 11, it came to light that his body produced insufficient amounts of growth hormones and he would likely always be short. A treatment was possible, but it was extremely expensive, and his parents were unable to afford it. Somehow the news of this misfortune spread to Barcelona officials, and a meeting was organized with Messi and his father that resulted in a contract being drafted on a napkin. It was official: Messi would join the ranks of the legendary team, and they would pay for the treatment.

Messi joined the youth academy and stayed there for a few years, playing with the reserve teams until 2004, when he was allowed to try his skills with the best. Since then, Messi has played close to 500 games with the team, scored almost 400 goals, and accumulated all possible accolades. His individual acknowledgments and honors are in the dozens, having four times won the award for best player in the world.

Messi's dream of becoming world champion with Argentina did not come to fruition at the 2014 World Cup in Brazil. Germany won in the extended final, and Messi and Argentina were forced to settle for a second place. Messi will be 31 years old in the next World Cup. Perhaps his dream will come true then.

Messi won the FIFA World Player of the Year Award/ Ballon d'Or in four consecutive years, from 2009 to 2013, the most of any player.

MÜLLER

Cunning

Thomas Müller will probably never forget the 2009–2010 season. He joined the first team of Bayern Munich, scored 19 goals in all tournaments, won both league and cup titles, and was a member of the runner-up team in the UEFA Champions League and the third-place team at the World Cup, where he was the top scorer and named the tournament's Best Young Player. However, the 2013–2014 season was even better. He scored 26 goals in all tournaments, became German champion and cup winner with Bayern, and celebrated a world championship with the German team. Müller was the 2014 World Cup's second top goal scorer with five goals and he was shortlisted for the Best Player of the Tournament.

Müller had scored a total of 10 goals in World Cup tournaments by the age of 25. The fact that almost half of his goals for the German team were scored in World Cup tournaments is very interesting. Müller is obviously at his best when the pressure is high.

Müller was only 10 years old when he joined Bayern Munich, and he has remained with the club since then and collected numerous awards. He is a tall and powerful forward and sometimes winger; he is diligent, has a fierce work ethic, and is constantly on the lookout for opportunities to score. Müller is not considered the world's most graceful forward, but he plays with passion and he always delivers results.

Müller describes his role on the soccer field as "Raumdeuter," which means "interpreter of space." By this he means that he continually strives to find gaps in the opposition's defense and utilize them by scoring himself or assisting others.

THOMAS MÜLLER
FORWARD
GERMANY

BORN SEPTEMBER 13, 1989
IN WEILHEIM, BAVARIA,
GERMANY
HEIGHT 6'1"
PLAYED ONLY FOR BAYERN
MUNICH
INTERNATIONAL GAMES 62
GOALS 26

MANUEL NEUER
GOALKEEPER
GERMANY

BORN MARCH 27, 1986
IN GELSENKIRCHEN, GERMANY
HEIGHT 6'4"
PLAYED FOR SCHALKE (GER)
AND BAYERN MUNICH (GER)
INTERNATIONAL GAMES 57

NEUER
Thinking Outside the Box!

Once in a blue moon a player enters the world stage who somehow alters the game of soccer through his brilliance or innovation. Manuel Neuer, goalkeeper for Germany and Bayern Munich, is such a player. For Neuer, defending the goal is not enough; instead he takes active part in his team's defensive strategy by taking on the position at the back of the defensive line. His style of play has attracted such attention that it called for an invention of a new term: "sweeper-keeper."

For some time, Neuer has been the greatest goalkeeper in the world. He is the incarnation of confidence in everything he engages with, and despite a strapping physique, his reflexes in the goal are terrifically sharp.

Neuer began playing with his hometown club Schalke at a very young age. When he was 19, Neuer was offered a contract with the club's senior team. Neuer won the DFB Cup with Schalke in 2011 and then transferred to Bayern Munich the following summer. With Bayern, Neuer's fame has risen to new heights, as proven by two league championships, two cup championships, and a victory in the UEFA Champions League.

In 2009, Neuer was selected by the coach of the German national team as third-string goalkeeper for the 2010 World Cup. Fate intervened and Neuer ended up as the main goalkeeper for the tournament and made his contribution to Germany's third-place finish. Four years later, and vastly more experienced, Neuer and his German companions took home the World Cup and he was chosen best goalkeeper of the tournament. Furthermore, he came in third, following Cristiano Ronaldo and Lionel Messi, for the Ballon d'Or in 2014, as player of the year. And it is no easy task for a goalkeeper to be considered among the list of top players.

Neuer is the second most expensive goalkeeper of all time. Bayern paid Schalke $27 million for him in 2011. That figure is topped only by the $45 million Juventus paid Parma for Italian Gianluigi Buffon in 2001.

NEYMAR DA SILVA
SANTOS JÚNIOR
FORWARD
BRAZIL

BORN FEBRUARY 5, 1992
IN MOGI DAS CRUZES, BRAZIL
HEIGHT 5'9"
PLAYED FOR SANTOS (BRS)
AND BARCELONA (ESP)
INTERNATIONAL GAMES 60
GOALS 42

NEYMAR
Speed and Energy

You need guts if you are going to compare a player to Pelé. Ever since Neymar da Silva Santos Júnior entered the world of soccer, comparisons have been drawn between him and the Black Pearl. And if that's not enough, Pelé has repeatedly exclaimed himself that Neymar is the world's greatest, superior to Lionel Messi and Cristiano Ronaldo. In the midst of these discussions, Neymar has done the only sensible thing: he has continued to develop as a soccer player.

Neymar began playing soccer on youth teams as a young boy. He enjoyed the support of his father, who also played soccer in his younger days. At the age of 11, Neymar joined Santos in São Paulo, and at 17, he signed a contract with the club and joined the senior team. During his first season, Neymar scored 14 goals in 48 matches (across all tournaments) and also added 19 assists. The following year was even better: 42 goals and 19 assists in 60 games. And so the story developed.

In 2013, Neymar sensed a desire for change, and soccer clubs around the world fought tooth and nail to sign him to a contract. Neymar eventually chose Barcelona and thereby became Messi's companion on the front lines of the Catalonian superteam. Neymar's performance during his first season with Barca was underwhelming, though he managed to score 15 goals. It was clear that all he needed was some time to adjust to the new circumstances, and in his second season, he exhibited vast improvements. On top of that, during the same time, the Barcelona team added the fantastic Luis Suárez.

Neymar flourished with the Brazilian national team in the 2013 Confederations Cup. He scored four goals in five games and was selected as the Golden Ball winner as the best player in the tournament. There were high expectations for the Brazilian team's performance at the 2014 World Cup. The team was considered exceptionally strong and therefore likely to succeed, on top of the fact that the team was playing on their home field. Neymar scored four goals during the group stages, and everything was heading in a positive direction. Neymar also scored the winning goal during the penalty shootout in a game against Chile in the round of 16. However, the hard blow came in the quarterfinal in a game against Colombia. Neymar was seriously injured close to the end of the match and was incapable of playing for the remainder of the tournament. Brazil lost 7–1 to the Germans in the semifinal.

Neymar shares his birthday with Cristiano Ronaldo, who is exactly seven years older.

PAUL POGBA
MIDFIELDER
FRANCE

BORN MARCH 15, 1993
IN LAGNY-SUR-MARNE,
OUTSIDE PARIS, FRANCE
HEIGHT 6'2"
PLAYED FOR MANCHESTER
UNITED (ENG) AND
JUVENTUS (ITA)
INTERNATIONAL GAMES 22
GOALS 5

POGBA
Oversight and Agility

Sir Alex Ferguson is the most celebrated soccer coach in the world. In his years with Manchester United he amassed numerous titles and coached many soccer players in their journey toward becoming the world's greatest, including Cristiano Ronaldo. However, Ferguson could also be remembered for not discovering the talents of Paul Pogba and allowing him to leave United.

The Frenchman is among the most promising soccer players to have entered the scene in recent years. Pogba is exceptionally powerful and ingenious, and he is gifted with a vast understanding of the game. After the 2012–2013 season, he was given the Golden Boy award as the best young player in Europe. The same honor was previously bestowed on players such as Wayne Rooney, Lionel Messi, Cesc Fàbregas, Sergio Agüero, Mario Balotelli, and Mario Götze.

Pogba, a son of immigrants from Guinea, was born and raised in a Parisian suburb. He played with a number of clubs as a child and adolescent and joined Manchester United when he was 16. Pogba played with all-French youth national teams and sometimes served as team captain. He led the victorious team at the 2013 U-20 World Cup, and in the same year he played for the first time with the senior national team.

Pogba played with Manchester United's senior team in the 2011–2012 season but made only seven appearances. The next summer, he joined the ranks of Juventus in Italy and was immediately given a more significant role on the powerful team that would become Italian champions in 2013 and 2014. Pogba is a dominant presence in the Italian giant's midfield and is poised to accomplish great things with France, too.

When Pogba was transferred from Le Havre to Manchester United as a teen, a conflict arose between the clubs. The French club accused the English one of "stealing" the player. United was cleared of all accusations of wrongdoing.

Pogba has older twin brothers who both play soccer professionally. One of them, Florentin Pogba, plays with the national team of their motherland, Guinea.

SERGIO RAMOS
DEFENDER
SPAIN

BORN MARCH 30, 1986
HEIGHT 6'
PLAYED FOR SEVILLA (ESP)
AND REAL MADRID (ESP)
INTERNATIONAL GAMES 124
GOALS 10

RAMOS
Raw Strength

Sergio Ramos has set a number of records throughout his career. He signed a contract with Real Madrid when he was 19 for the highest amount of money ever paid by a Spanish club for such a young player. Ramos became the youngest player of all time to play 100 matches with the Spanish national team, and he has received the most red cards in Real's lengthy history.

An abundance of records notwithstanding, Sergio Ramos is also a fantastic soccer player. Ramos is unyielding on defense, and the world's fiercest forwards struggle to find ways to get past him. Ramos has a keen eye for the goal to boot. When the going gets rough, Ramos is usually first to appear on the front lines of Real's offense, and woe to the defender who loses sight of Ramos inside the penalty area.

As a child, Ramos played with Sevilla and was a member of the senior team in the premier league before the Madrid powerhouse acquired him in 2005. Ever since, Ramos has been part of the starting lineup for Real Madrid and has rarely missed a match, except, of course, for the times when he has actually been barred from playing.

Ramos's career is dotted with accolades, including three Spanish league titles; two Copa del Rey titles; and victory in the UEFA Champions League, UEFA Super Cup, and world champion in the FIFA Club World Cup. And this is only half the story. Ramos has played with the Spanish national team since 2005 and won the UEFA European Championship in 2008 and 2012 and then became world champion at the 2010 World Cup. During Spain's humiliating 2014 World Cup, Ramos was the only defender that the coach trusted enough to participate in every match of the tournament. That fact speaks volumes about Ramos.

Ramos has scored 4 to 7 goals in each of his seasons with Real Madrid. Even some forwards have a hard time reaching that level.

FRANCK RIBÉRY
WINGMAN
FRANCE

BORN APRIL 7, 1983
IN BOULOGNE-SUR-MER, NEAR
CALAIS, FRANCE
HEIGHT 5'7"
PLAYED FOR METZ (FRA),
GALATASARAY (TUR),
MARSEILLE (FRA), AND BAYERN
MUNICH (GER)
INTERNATIONAL GAMES 81
GOALS 16

RIBÉRY
The Rough Diamond

The "Jewel of French Soccer" was the moniker given to Franck Ribéry by one of the world's greatest players, Zinedine Zidane. When Zidane speaks, the world of soccer listens. Contrary to most well-known soccer players, in his younger days, Ribéry wasn't considered exceptional in any way. He played with a few clubs in the lower divisions of French soccer and developed slowly but surely. At around the age of 20, he was laboring as a construction worker alongside his father.

Eventually, Ribéry joined Metz in the first division in 2004. He stayed with Metz for a few months, then transferred to Galatasaray in Turkey, where he collected his first title: the Turkish Cup. After that, Ribéry returned once again to France, this time joining Marseille, where he played for two seasons before being purchased by German giants Bayern Munich in 2007, where he has remained since and has become a key player, contributing greatly to the team's success. With Bayern, Ribéry was properly able to express himself as a player; he finally became a prolific goal scorer and he has hoarded numerous titles and individual accolades, for example winning Player of the Year in Germany. Moreover, Ribéry has been named to the Team of the Year on numerous occasions.

Ribéry played with the French national team for the first time in 2005 and was a member of the second-place team at the 2006 World Cup. He is fast, extremely tricky, and unpredictable, and at his best he is a true joy to watch.

Ribéry has large scars on his face. When he was two years old, he and his family were in a serious car accident. He has refused to have the scars removed with plastic surgery. "The scars are part of me, and people will just have to take me the way I am," he says.

ARJEN ROBBEN
WINGER
NETHERLANDS

BORN JANUARY 23, 1984
IN BEDUM, NETHERLANDS
HEIGHT 5'11"
PLAYED FOR PSV EINDHOVEN
(HOL), CHELSEA (ENG),
GRONINGEN (HOL), REAL
MADRID (ESP), AND BAYERN
MUNICH (GER)
INTERNATIONAL GAMES 86
GOALS 28

As Robben sweeps in from the right wing with the ball glued to his feet, drawing ever closer to the opponent's goal, the whole world knows his next moves. He cuts the ball to the inside of the left foot and shoots it in an arc toward the far corner. But knowing the strategy makes it no less stoppable, as Robben's catalog of goals scored in this manner will attest.

ROBBEN
Searching for the Winning Goal

Arjen Robben is a true champion. He has played in four different countries and won championship titles in all of them. Few boast such achievements—maybe aside from Zlatan Ibrahimović!

At 16, Robben's professional career began with Groningen in the Netherlands. He joined PSV when he was 18 and became Dutch champion with the club in his first season. Additionally, he was selected Talent of the Year. Two years later, Robben traveled to England. Manchester United had made an offer for him that PSV Eindhoven officials considered disgraceful. The news spread to Chelsea, which jumped at the opportunity and produced a sum more pleasing to the Dutch club.

Robben won the Premier League championship with Chelsea, but his goal scoring decreased throughout his time with the club. Nevertheless, Robben performed well, and in 2007 he signed a contract with the Spanish megateam Real Madrid, where he stayed for two seasons, winning the Spanish league championship.

Robben thrived in Madrid and was dissatisfied when club officials decided to transfer him to Bayern Munich in order to make room for Cristiano Ronaldo and Kaká. Robben's response was one of a true athlete: he became a better and better player. His stint with the German team is characterized by sheer dominance: three league championships, three cup championships, and a UEFA Champions League title.

Robben played his first international game in 2003, and over time he became one of the key players on the Dutch team, which is one of the world's greatest. With the Dutch national team, Robben landed in second place at the 2010 World Cup and came in third at the 2014 World Cup. Robben was an integral part of the team in both tournaments. He is incredibly agile and clever, gifted with meticulous ball control, and possesses a precision shot. In addition, Robben has laser focus and he continuously hunts for the perfect goal opportunity.

Robben has made major contributions to the successes of Bayern in recent years, sometimes winning matches on his own accord. He has frequently been accused of diving in order to fish for a penalty kick, but he is surely not the only one guilty of such theatrics.

JAMES RODRIGUEZ
ATTACKING MIDFIELDER
COLOMBIA

BORN JULY 12, 1991
IN CÚCUTA, COLOMBIA
HEIGHT 5'11"
PLAYED FOR BANFIELD (ARG),
PORTO (POR), MONACO (FRA),
AND REAL MADRID (ESP)
INTERNATIONAL GAMES 32
GOALS 12

RODRÍGUEZ
Colombian Wunderkind

The journey from a small city in the Andes to one of the most magnificent soccer stadiums in the world, Santiago Bernabéu Stadium in Madrid, seems like a long one.

James Rodríguez undertook precisely that journey, though the travels were relatively speedy. At 16 he played in the league of the greatest in his home country; at 17 and 18 he played in Argentina; at 19 he traveled to Porto in Portugal; at 22 he moved to Monaco in France; and at 23 he continued on to Real Madrid in Spain, the most triumphant soccer club in the world.

Rodríguez's journey is also strewn with awards and honors. He became Argentinean and Portuguese champion (three times) and was selected Best Young Player in Argentina, Best Young Player in the Copa Libertadores (South American championship), and Player of the Year in Portugal. Rodríguez won his biggest individual victories at the 2014 World Cup in Brazil, becoming the tournament's top goal scorer with six goals in five matches. Moreover, one of his goals was chosen Goal of the Tournament and he was named to the World Cup all-star team.

Rodríguez's volleyed first goal against Uruguay was described as "one of the greatest goals the World Cup had ever seen" by Óscar Tabárez, the coach of Uruguay, who also called Rodríguez the "best player in the World Cup." Despite Rodríguez's tearful disappointment when the Colombian team was knocked out of the quarterfinal, he and the rest of the national team earned the right to be proud of their performance in the tournament.

Rodríguez is considered one of the most promising players to enter the world soccer stage in recent years. The price paid by Real for Rodríguez confirms this—a whopping $108 million, making him the fifth most expensive player in soccer history. Any fear of Rodríguez falling in the shadow of the other Real superstars turned out to be unwarranted, as he has assuredly proven his worth. In his first season with Real, he alternated between the position of winger and attacking midfielder. By this point, he was no longer the Colombian wunderkind; Rodríguez has soared to the upper echelons of the world's soccer legends.

> "For me, special talents are those who do things that are completely out of the ordinary. Diego Maradona, Lionel Messi, Luis Suárez, James Rodríguez—they do things because they have certain [unique] gifts that make them special." —Óscar Tabárez

CRISTIANO RONALDO DOS
SANTOS AVEIRO
FORWARD
PORTUGAL

BORN FEBRUARY 5, 1985
IN FUNCHAL, MADEIRA,
PORTUGAL
HEIGHT 6'1"
PLAYED FOR SPORTING (POR),
MANCHESTER UNITED (ENG),
AND REAL MADRID (ESP)
INTERNATIONAL GAMES 118
GOALS 52

Ronaldo does not have tattoos
because it would prevent him
from donating blood, which he
does several times a year.

RONALDO
Powerful and Versatile Goal Scorer

Some would've turned bitter. In the spring of 2008, Cristiano Ronaldo was 23 years old. He was the major catalyst in Manchester United's victory at the UEFA Champions League and the English Premier League. He racked up the goals with great swiftness and power. He triumphantly hoisted the golden ball and seemed on his way to becoming an annual subscriber to the award, especially after joining Real Madrid, the most renowned and victorious team in the world. Ronaldo was unrivaled and there was no indication that this would change.

However, all of a sudden there was trouble in paradise. Ronaldo continued his victorious march with Real and goal-scoring figures steadily rose, but suddenly a young Argentine rival cropped up. Two years Ronaldo's junior, the super-agile genius named Lionel Messi was there to stay—and he managed to snatch the Golden Ball the following four years in a row! Everyone agreed about and recognized Ronald's brilliance but he could no longer be called the best. Yes, some would've turned bitter.

Yet, Ronaldo did not. The competition with Messi injected Ronaldo with spirit and through tireless training and incredible ambition, Ronaldo eventually surpassed his worthy opponent.

Ronaldo's awards are in abundance, almost countless, and once Messi's monopoly over the Golden Ball came to an end, Ronaldo managed to snatch it away from him, winning them two times in a row, in 2013 and 2014.

Once again, he's the world's greatest. That is the biggest achievement of the genius Christano Ronaldo!

Ronaldo's father named his son after the American president Ronald Reagan.

ALEXIS SÁNCHEZ
FORWARD
CHILE

BORN DECEMBER 19, 1988
IN TOCOPILLA, CHILE
HEIGHT 5'6½"
PLAYED FOR COBRELOA (CHL),
UDINESE (ITA), BARCELONA
(ESP), AND ARSENAL (ENG)
INTERNATIONAL GAMES 77
GOALS 26

SÁNCHEZ
The Fearless Attacker

Alexis Sánchez was born in Tocopilla, in the northernmost part of Chile, and he is the best-known product of the village. Sánchez joined his hometown club Cobreloa when he was 16 years old and was purchased by the Italian club Udinese only a year later. Quickly after he joined Udinese, Sánchez was loaned, first to Colo-Colo in Chile and then to River Plate in Argentina. Udinese (like many other clubs) loans promising players to other clubs in order for them to gain experience. Sánchez did well with both clubs, winning championships in both Chile and Argentina. He then played three seasons with Udinese in the Italian league and scored 12 goals in his final season with the team. In 2011, he signed a contract with Spanish giants Barcelona, with whom he became cup champion in 2012 and league champion in 2013. Sánchez claimed he had two goals when he arrived at Barcelona: to learn from geniuses such as Lionel Messi and Xavi and to facilitate more victories for the team. Both goals came to fruition.

Aside from gathering titles, Sánchez experienced other unforgettable moments with Barca. He scored a goal in his first top league match, he scored the winning goal in one of the El Clásico games against Real Madrid, and during his final season, he scored 21 goals, a personal best.

In the summer of 2014, Sánchez was sold to Arsenal in England, becoming the second most expensive player in the club's history, following Mesut Özil. Sánchez paid off immediately, as his attacking spirit, speed, and fearlessness delivered a host of goals and assists for Arsenal.

Sánchez has been one of the key players for the aggressive and entertaining national Chilean national team over the past years. He participated for the club in the 2010 and 2014 World Cups.

Barcelona forwards, led by Messi, were fierce to the degree that Sánchez fell slightly into the shadows, and some claimed that his stretch with the Catalonian team was a failure. To the contrary: he scored 39 goals in 88 league matches over a period of three years, almost a goal for every two games. That counts as world-class performance on such a powerful team.

SILVA

The Classy Winger

David Silva hails from the village of Arguineguín on the sunny Canary Islands and began playing soccer early in his youth. Strangely enough, this short but agile player was originally a goalkeeper, but he was soon moved to the wing. At the age of 14, Silva was offered a contract to join the ranks of Valencia, where he matured as a player. Valencia officials were acutely aware of Silva's promise and also knew how to extract the talent to the most productive degree possible. After a period on loan with two different clubs, Silva was brought back to Valencia and played with the team from 2006 to 2010. He played on the wing and exhibited great agility and attacking spirit. Silva's cooperation with the goal hoarder David Villa is renowned. The team also featured other great players such as Juan Mata.

Silva was chosen for the Spanish national team in 2006, and was a member of the UEFA Champions League championship teams in 2008 and 2012. He became world champion in 2010. Following the 2010 World Cup, Silva changed course and joined the English club Manchester City. During his first season with the team, Manchester City took home the cup title, and they would go on to win the league championship in 2012 and 2014.

Silva has increasingly developed as a key player with Man City, his fame growing on a dangerous and dominant team. He scores more goals than ever and is, on a good day, a jack-of-all-trades in the team's offensive play. Silva's performance for the national team was at first slightly overshadowed by the midfield geniuses Xavi and Iniesta, but he gradually came into his own and is now a significant contributor to the team's midfield strategy

Silva is a master at retaining possession and creating space for himself and his teammates to open up a defense.

Silva earned the nickname "Merlin" for his dazzling footwork and ability to create plays out of thin air.

DAVID SILVA
WINGER/ATTACKING
MIDFIELDER
SPAIN

BORN JANUARY 8, 1986
IN ARGUINEGUIN, SPAIN
HEIGHT 5'8"
PLAYED FOR VALENCIA (ESP)
AND MANCHESTER CITY (ENG)
INTERNATIONAL GAMES 87
GOALS 22

RAHEEM STERLING
WINGER/ATTACKING
MIDFIELDER/FORWARD
ENGLAND

BORN DECEMBER 8, 1994
IN KINGSTON, JAMAICA
HEIGHT 5'7"
PLAYED ONLY FOR LIVERPOOL
INTERNATIONAL GAMES 14
GOALS 1

STERLING
Cunning, Quick, Attacking Spirit

Raheem Sterling is one of the most promising players to arise in English soccer in a long time. In fact, Sterling harbors such promise that Xavi himself claimed that the midfielder has everything it takes to play with Barcelona.

Sterling was born in Jamaica but moved to London when he was five years old. From the age of nine, he played with the youth academy of London club Queens Park Rangers. In 2009, he signed a contract with Liverpool. There, Sterling matured as a player under the guidance of celebrated captain Steven Gerrard. Sterling was only 17 years old when he played his first game with Liverpool's senior team, joining the starting lineup during the 2012–2013 season.

Sterling became an important link in Liverpool's fantastic front line with Daniel Sturridge and Luis Suárez. Following Suárez's departure, Sterling's responsibility rose in proportion, at barely 20 years of age.

It is clear that if Liverpool is capable of holding on to this boundlessly gifted young man, he could ascend to become one of the club's greatest players ever, and there is certainly no lack of giants in the history of the five-time European champions. However, as Xavi's words show, other big teams' interest in Sterling is awakening. Sterling is quick, agile, and cunning; he has excellent ball control and is a danger around the opponent's goal. And he will soon become a key player on the English national team, along with his Liverpool companion Sturridge.

Sterling grew up with his grandmother in Jamaica but then moved with his mother to England. His absent father was murdered when the boy was only nine years old.

LUIS SUÁREZ
FORWARD
URUGUAY

BORN JANUARY 24, 1987
IN SALTO, URUGUAY
HEIGHT 5'11"
PLAYED FOR NACIONAL (URU),
GRONINGEN (HOL), AJAX
(HOL), LIVERPOOL (ENG), AND
BARCELONA (ESP)
INTERNATIONAL GAMES 82
GOALS 43

SUÁREZ
A Flawed Genius

The man from Uruguay, Luis Suárez is one of the world's most celebrated contemporary soccer players. Unfortunately, it is not solely due to his talents as an athlete and goal scorer. Suárez is a working-class man and learned soccer on the streets, first in his hometown of Salto and then in Uruguay's capital, Montevideo. His magnificent skills were manifest from early on and so was his stalwart fighting spirit, which sometimes got him into trouble.

At a young age, Suárez traveled to Europe and made a name for himself with Ajax in the Netherlands. Next, he was transferred to Liverpool in England and his performance there attracted worldwide attention. Suárez is a true magician with the ball, almost absurdly agile, and he tirelessly seeks pathways to the opponent's goal. His vision on the field is so extensive that he sees paths that others cannot.

Suárez's incredible performance with Liverpool made him into a god in the eyes of soccer fans around the world. But fans were forced to overlook certain events in his career, such as when Suárez bit an opponent—on more than on occasion—or got himself entangled in other conflicts.

In summer 2014, Suárez was suspended and banned from playing soccer after he bit his opponent during the 2014 World Cup in Brazil. He made use of the time and transferred to Barcelona, where he plays at the side of Lionel Messi and Neymar—a dangerous front lineup, to say the very least. But Suárez also used the time to sort himself out, and now he seems like a more mature player than he was previously—and prepared to allow his talents to grow even further.

During the 2013–2014 season, Suárez scored 31 goals in 33 league matches for Liverpool and nearly helped his team to a long-awaited championship title. Liverpool coach Brendan Rodgers said about Suárez: "He has shown in his time at Liverpool in the last year or so that he is near unplayable. He on his own can occupy a back four with his movement and his cleverness."

YAYA TOURÉ
MIDFIELDER
IVORY COAST

BORN MAY 13, 1993
IN BOUAKÉ, IVORY COAST
HEIGHT 6'2"
PLAYED FOR BEVEREN (BEL),
METALLURG DONETSK (UKR),
OLYMPIACOS (GRC), MONACO
(FRA), BARCELONA (ESP), AND
MANCHESTER CITY (ENG)
INTERNATIONAL GAMES 95
GOALS 19